The Jelly Bean Machine

Kelly Doudna

Consulting Editor, Diane Craig, M.A./Reading Specialist

ABDO Publishing Company

Published by ABDO Publishing Company, 4940 Viking Drive, Edina, Minnesota 55435.

Printed in the United States.

Credits
Edited by: Pam Price
Curriculum Coordinator: Nancy Tuminelly
Cover and Interior Design and Production: Mighty Media
Photo and Illustration Credits: BananaStock Ltd., Comstock, Corbis Images, Digital Vision, Kelly Doudna, Eyewire Images, Hemera, Stockbyte

Library of Congress Cataloging-in-Publication Data

Doudna, Kelly, 1963-
    The jelly bean machine / Kelly Doudna.
        p. cm. -- (Rhyme time)
    Includes index.
    ISBN 1-59197-795-9 (hardcover)
    ISBN 1-59197-901-3 (paperback)
    1. English language--Rhyme--Juvenile literature. I. Title. II. Rhyme time (ABDO Publishing Company)

PE1517.D6835 2005
808.1--dc22
                                                                    2004049041

SandCastle™ books are created by a professional team of educators, reading specialists, and content developers around five essential components that include phonemic awareness, phonics, vocabulary, text comprehension, and fluency. All books are written, reviewed, and leveled for guided reading, early intervention reading, and Accelerated Reader® programs and designed for use in shared, guided, and independent reading and writing activities to support a balanced approach to literacy instruction.

Let Us Know

After reading the book, SandCastle would like you to tell us your stories about reading. What is your favorite page? Was there something hard that you needed help with? Share the ups and downs of learning to read. We want to hear from you! To get posted on the ABDO Publishing Company Web site, send us e-mail at:

sandcastle@abdopub.com

SandCastle Level: Fluent

Words that rhyme do not have to be spelled the same. These words rhyme with each other:

bean

mean

canteen

queen

clean

scene

green

screen

lean

teen

3

Ethan is eating a blue jelly bean.

When they go hiking, Joey and his dad bring a **canteen**.

Lauren and Isabella work together to clean the car.

Jessie's sweater is green.

Brianna and Holly make towers that are straight.

They do not **lean**.

Taylor pretends to be a dancing queen.

Tony pretends to be **mean**.

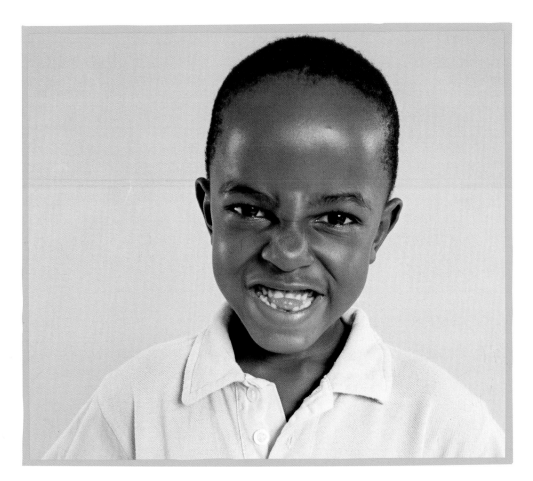

Kayla points to her computer screen.

John and Brandon are at the movies.

They laugh at a funny **scene**.

Christopher is twelve years old.
Next year he will be a **teen**.

The Jelly Bean Machine

Colleen the teen
wanted a jelly bean.

In a room
that was clean,
she spied
an odd-looking
green machine.

15

Colleen turned on the machine and looked at the screen.

On the screen she saw a scene of a beautiful queen.

16

The queen on the screen
had a green jelly bean.

Colleen thought, "This must mean that I can use this machine to make another green jelly bean."

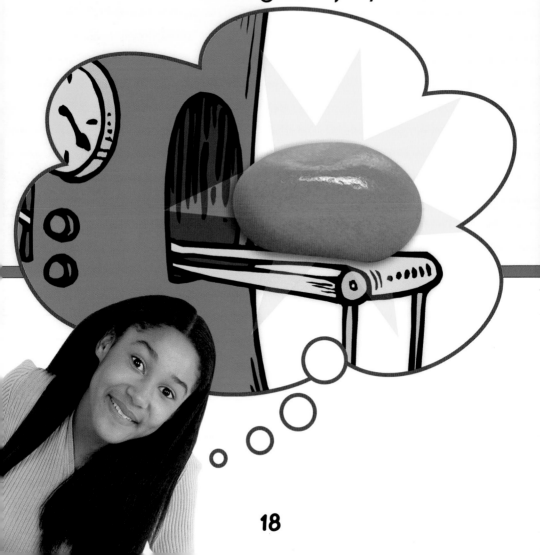

1, 2, 3, 4, 5, 6, 7,
8, 9, 10, 11, 12,
13, 14, 15 !

She counted to fifteen
while the machine
did things unseen.

When the machine
finished its routine,
out came bean after bean.

Soon the pile was so high
that Colleen the teen
could barely be seen.

She exclaimed,
"I love this jelly bean machine!"

Rhyming Riddle

What do you call a high-school student who just took a bath?

Clean teen

Glossary

canteen. a container for carrying water while hiking or camping

lean. to move or bend from an upright position

spy. to catch sight of

teen. a teenage person

tower. a structure or building that is much taller than it is wide

unseen. out of sight or not noticed

About SandCastle™

A professional team of educators, reading specialists, and content developers created the SandCastle™ series to support young readers as they develop reading skills and strategies and increase their general knowledge. The SandCastle™ series has four levels that correspond to early literacy development in young children. The levels are provided to help teachers and parents select the appropriate books for young readers.

Emerging Readers
(no flags)

Beginning Readers
(1 flag)

Transitional Readers
(2 flags)

Fluent Readers
(3 flags)

These levels are meant only as a guide. All levels are subject to change.

ABDO
Publishing Company

To see a complete list of SandCastle™ books and other nonfiction titles from ABDO Publishing Company, visit www.abdopub.com or contact us at:
4940 Viking Drive, Edina, Minnesota 55435 • 1-800-800-1312 • fax: 1-952-831-1632